# MY HISTORY
# Scrapbook

Selma Montford

**Wayland**

# My History Scrapbook

Editor: Kate Asser
Book designer: Loraine Hayes

First published in 1993 by
Wayland (Publishers) Ltd
61 Western Road, Hove
East Sussex BN3 1JD, England

© Copyright 1993 Wayland (Publishers) Ltd

**British Library Cataloguing in Publication Data**

Montford, Selma
  My History Scrapbook
  I. Title
  907

**HARDBACK** ISBN 0 7502 0378 1
**PAPERBACK** ISBN 0 7502 0602 0

Typeset by DJS Fotoset Ltd, Brighton, Sussex, England
Printed in Italy by G. Canale & C.S.p.A, Turin.

**Picture acknowledgements**

The publishers would like to thank the following for allowing their pictures to be reproduced in this book: Chapel Studios p21 (above), p24, p36, p37; Lewis Cohen Urban Studies Centre *Cover top left*, p5 (below); East Sussex County Library *Contents page (below)*, p14, p15, p39; East Sussex Records Office p19 (below); Catherine Ellis p41 (above), p42 (below), p43 (above and middle); Mary Evans p43 (below); Eye Ubiquitous *Cover top centre-left*, *Cover bottom right*, p4, p16, p28; The Mansell Collection p25 (above); Archie Miles *title page*, p17; Tony Stone Worldwide p5, p12, p21 (below); Topham Picture Source p8, p10, p19 (above), p20, p22, p23, p30, p31, p32, p40; Wayland Picture Library *Cover top centre-right, top right, bottom left, bottom centre-left, bottom centre-bottom, Contents page (top and centre)*, p18, p26, p27, p41 (below), p42 (above), p43 (below), p44, p45; Tim Woodcock *Cover bottom centre-top*, p6, p9, p13, p25 (below), p29. All artwork is by Deborah Kindred. A selection of Bewick engravings from the Dover Pictorial Archive Series has been used.

Thanks are also due to Cupernham School, Romsey, and Plincke Landscape, Winchester.

# Contents

All the words that appear in **bold** are explained in the glossary.

# Your place in history

History is not only about kings and queens, the rich and famous, parliaments and politics – it is also about ordinary people and their lives. Local history is about where you live and your family is part of the history of your area.

History is the story of the past based on evidence of different kinds. It does not have to be a long time ago. Yesterday is history today and today will be history tomorrow.

Your history started the day you were born. Ask your parents for your birth certificate. This document gives the evidence of your date and place of birth.

The history of your family started long before the date on your birth certificate. Have you any family photograph albums with pictures of your older relatives as children? What do your parents and grandparents remember about their parents?

## Your house

The history of your house started when it was built, but the history of the place where it was built probably started many years or **centuries** before that. Who lived in your house before you? What was on the land before it was built? If it is an old

**You and your family are helping to make the history of your local area.**

house you may find it on old maps. If it was built before the mid-1970s you may find it in old street directories, like the one on the right. These recorded people's names, addresses and sometimes what they did for a living. They were used like modern telephone directories. Directories and maps can be found in your local reference library.

## Signs of the past

If you look around you carefully at the place where you live, you can find out a lot about the past. Look at the buildings that are still standing, as well as the spaces between them. Try walking around the same streets in different directions and at different times of day. As the light changes you may see things you have not noticed before, such as marks and lettering on the walls. You might take these familiar buildings for granted, but they contain many secrets about life in the past.

**WHAT'S THE EVIDENCE?**
- look at your birth certificate
- can you find your house on an old map?
- see if your house is included in a street directory

# Local history begins at home

Before you can start to investigate the past, you need to know which area or subject you are going to investigate. It is a good idea to start close to home – perhaps even with your home. You may like to take a larger area, for example a group of houses including your own house or flat, or your street. You might study a group of shops, or your **neighbourhood**, village or **suburb**. It would be better to be curious about a small area first, or you might find there is too much evidence for you to uncover.

## Make a date of it

If you are starting with your own house or flat, you need to know when it was built. Ask your parents if they have a copy of the deeds. This is the document which records when a building was sold to a new owner.

If your house was built before the mid-1970s, you could try to find it in the street directories for your town. The date of the street directory in which your house is first mentioned will probably be about a year after it was built. Can you find out when your house first appeared on street maps with a large **scale?** Remember that maps are usually a few years out of date even when they are first printed, as they take some years to make.

**The houses in this street are all slightly different.**

# My House

**WHERE TO LOOK:**
- check the deeds of your house if you can
- when did the first street directory include your house?
- is your house on large-scale street maps?
- see if your house was first advertised for sale in old editions of the local paper

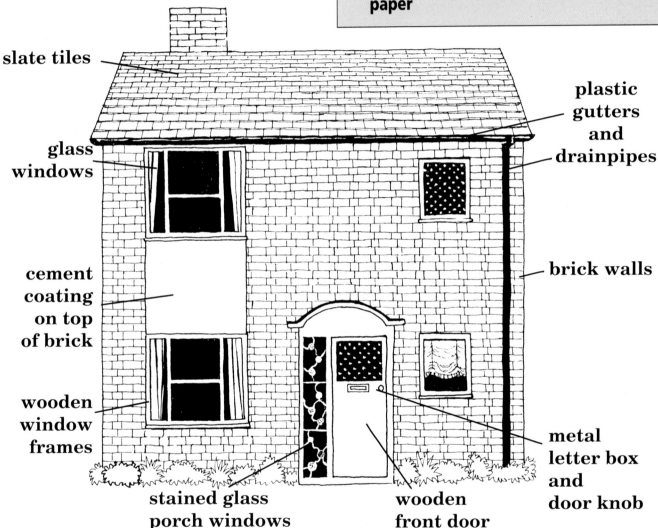

slate tiles

plastic gutters and drainpipes

glass windows

cement coating on top of brick

brick walls

wooden window frames

stained glass porch windows

wooden front door

metal letter box and door knob

You may be able to find the very first advertisement offering your house for sale in a past edition of your local paper.

## Putting on the style

Try drawing your home from memory. Pretend that you are writing a letter to someone who is coming to visit you for the first time. Show in your drawing the different materials that make up your house. If your house is the same as all the others in the street, you will have to try to think of details which would help a stranger to identify it.

# Houses and homes

What sort of house do you live in? You might live in a terraced house, which is one of a row of three or more houses joined together. If your house is one of a terrace of houses, two or three storeys high, it is called a town house. A bungalow is a single-storey house, and can be detached (standing on its own) or semi-detached (joined to another house on one side). Flats are several one-floor homes in one building. This could be an old building converted into flats, a purpose-built modern block, or a high-rise block. Maisonettes are flats built on two floors.

**A lot of families can live in a single block of flats. They all share the gardens outside.**

Until they have weathered, newly-built houses seem to sit on top of the land rather than be a part of it.

## Changing fashion

Houses built within a few **decades** of each other look quite similar. This is because a particular building style was fashionable then. Some styles are named after the person who ruled the country at that time. Edwardian houses date from the reign of Edward VII (1901-1910) and Victorian houses from the reign of Queen Victoria (1837-1901). Most buildings

You might photograph your own house or draw some of the details of it, to show how it fits in with its neighbours. Can you decide from your pictures what style it is? You might mark your drawing or photograph with notes around the edge, perhaps describing things which you cannot draw, or which do not show up on the photograph.

built before Victorian times are grouped into **Regency** (1811-20), **Georgian** (1714-1830), **Stuart** (1603-1714) and **Tudor** (1485-1603) styles. Buildings built before Tudor times belong to the **Middle Ages** and are called Medieval.

## Old and new

The houses in a street are usually the same type and age. If you find a modern house in a street of older houses, you should be curious about what it has replaced. It might have replaced an older house, like the remaining ones in the street, or it could be built in the grounds of a large house. Why was there space for the new house? It could have been built on the site of a **market garden** or orchard, or on the site where a house had been bombed in the Second World War.

New buildings have a raw look. They seem to sit on top of the ground rather than belong to it. If they are houses with gardens, the trees and bushes will be young and small. Some new houses imitate the styles of the past, so you can be tricked into thinking that a house is older than it is. Some new houses will have enormous chimneys, and some will not have a chimney at all – they may have a small pipe or square box on the wall instead.

If a building is old it will look weathered and may have moss on the roof, or lichen on the walls. The steps may be worn down, or the roof may have been patched with newer materials. The number of chimney pots there are on top of an old house will tell you how many rooms there are inside it. Do you know why?

**The houses in this Yorkshire village were built so close together that the washing had to be dried in the street.**

# Houses Through History

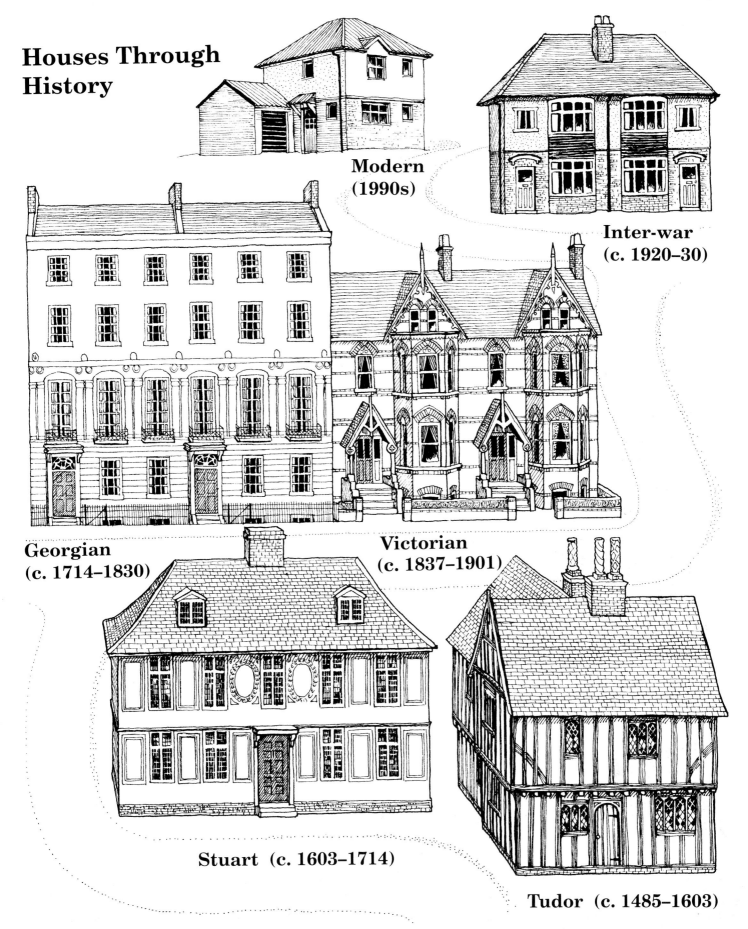

Modern
(1990s)

Inter-war
(c. 1920–30)

Georgian
(c. 1714–1830)

Victorian
(c. 1837–1901)

Stuart  (c. 1603–1714)

Tudor  (c. 1485–1603)

## Into the past

Houses built since the Second World War are called post-war houses. Tower blocks were built in the 1960s and 1970s, but not many high-rise flats are built now as many people do not like to live in them. They are not suitable for young children or old people.

Houses built between the two world wars (1918-39) are called inter-war houses. They often have corner windows or curved corners and curved windows with metal frames. Their trees and bushes will have grown, making the houses look as if they are part of the ground on which they are built. The **casement windows** will have small panes of glass. Watch out though, you may be tricked, because many people have replaced the windows of old houses with new, large panes of glass. Your clue for detecting new windows is the material of the window frames. The original ones will have been made of wood or metal, but the replacement ones will probably be of plastic. Imitation Tudor houses were also built between the wars. They look neat and have wooden beams stuck onto the outside for decoration.

**This inter-war building in Glasgow was once a hotel. It is built in the art deco style popular in the 1930s.**

**A Georgian terrace in Wisbech, Cambridgeshire, showing how the windows are smaller at the top of the house.**

Edwardian houses, built at the beginning of this century, are usually red brick and are often in terraces, though some are detached. Sometimes they are decorated with patterns in the brickwork, or on the **lintels** above the **sash windows**. Many have small front gardens with low walls, railings and pillars.

Victorian houses, from the second half of the last century, are usually more richly-decorated than Edwardian houses. Some of them may have a coating of stucco, or cement, on the outside. They usually have roofs made of **slate** from Wales, brought in by steam train.

A few towns, such as Bath, have Regency houses built in squares, or crescents and terraces. These date from the beginning of the nineteenth century. They are often decorated with balconies and canopies.

Georgian houses, built in the eighteenth century, are usually built of brick and have tile roofs. They are simple and **symmetrical** to look at. The sash windows have small panes and those windows nearest the roof are smaller than the rest. Do you know why? There may be a parapet, or low wall, built around the edge of the roof. You may think that a Georgian house looks like a doll's house.

Stuart and Tudor houses were built in the fifteenth and sixteenth centuries. Some were built around a framework of wooden beams, like Medieval houses. The beams are uneven and can be seen from the outside. Sometimes the first floor hangs out over the ground floor, in what is called a jetty. Other houses were built of brick or stone. Sometimes they have tall chimneys, built in a complicated spiralling pattern, and roofs of clay tile, stone tile or thatch. Remember that the roof, windows and doors that you see today may not be the original ones.

**The jetties and wooden framework of this fifteenth-century building are clear to see.**

**WHAT ARE THE CLUES?**
- **what are the windows and their frames like?**
- **what size are the panes of glass?**
- **how old are the plants in the garden?**
- **is your home decorated with beams of wood, patterns in the brickwork, or stucco?**
- **what is your house built of?**
- **does your home have a balcony or canopy?**
- **see if your home has a wooden frame that shows through to the outside**

# Rich and poor

The examples we have of houses from the eighteenth century and before often belonged to the noblemen who owned most of the land. Some poorer people owned their own small farms, but many worked for the nobles, in their houses or fields. These people often lived in the attics of the nobles' houses or in tiny cottages on the land.

You will see that there was also a great difference between the way poor and wealthy people lived in towns. For example, during the Industrial Revolution in the nineteenth century (see p. 20), thousands of houses were built for all the workers around the new mills, mines, shipyards and factories. They were small and close together, with back yards instead of gardens. The rich owners of the mills, mines and factories, on the other hand, had large, elegant houses. However, when you see the large houses, remember that not all those who lived in them lived in luxury. Do not forget to look at the parts of a large house, such as the attics and basement, where the servants lived and worked.

**Could you guess that these cottages were built by the coast, close to a pebble beach?**

# Streets

It is not only the houses in a street that can tell you about the past. The style of street furniture has also changed with time. Street furniture is everything, such as signs, railings, street lights and benches, found in a street. Street furniture can tell you about transport, how buildings were heated, entertainment, work, wars and people.

Street signs have changed over the years. The oldest were carved into a wall. Later on, some were made of blue tiles. Signposts may be on a pole, on a wall, or on a street lamp. Sometimes street names can help the historian. A street named Trafalgar Street was probably built just after the battle of Trafalgar in 1805, and a road called Mill Road probably led to the site of an old mill.

▲ This building post is very useful as it tells you when the building was put up and who was running the town at the time.

You would be able to guess roughly when this bench was built because it is decorated with the face of Queen Victoria.▶

**WHAT TO LOOK FOR:**
- signposts and street signs
- railings and ironwork
- street lights
- benches
- posts, bollards and markers
- different kinds of pavement
- cobbles and setts
- post boxes
- coal hole covers
- bus or tram shelters
- horse troughs

**When do you think that this post box was built? Can you see the clue?** ▶

Look out for different kinds of **boundary stones**, **bollards** and **tethering posts**. Look for pavements of different materials – they might be of brick, stone or **asphalt**. If the **tarmac** on the road is worn away, you may see wooden or stone blocks showing through. Granite **setts** were used in places where horses might slip, for example, at the arched entrance to a **coaching inn**, a **mews** or yard.

Post boxes show the initials of whoever was king or queen when the post box was made. Can you find a post box with 'VR' for *Victoria Regina* on it, which is Latin for 'In the reign of Queen Victoria'? The buildings in a street with a Victorian post box will probably also be Victorian.

In older streets you may find coal hole covers in the pavement outside each house. Coal for fires was delivered through the hole, into the cellar underneath. The cover will sometimes give the name of the local **foundry** where it was made. You may find the same name on street lamps or park benches.

**Tram** and bus shelters tell you where the tram and bus routes went. The longest shelters are on the busiest routes, which had longer queues.

Statues are usually of rich or famous people, but the names of all those who died in the world wars, both rich and poor, will be on **war memorials**.

Can you find a horse trough? Until about fifty years ago, many carts were still drawn by horses, which needed water to drink.

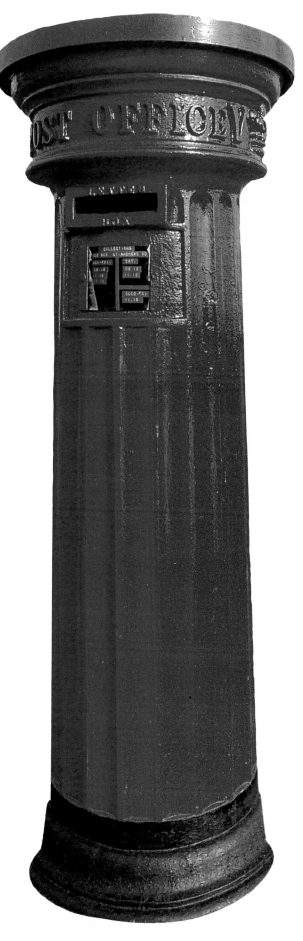

# Where you live

Do you know why your town, village or neighbourhood was built where it is? Is it on high ground, which would have been easy to defend? Did it grow up near a well, or a spring, or where a river could be crossed? In the reference library there may be **aerial photographs** of where you live, which will show up these features clearly. Compare the photographs with what you can see for yourself outside.

Your reference library will have a **geology** map of your area, showing the different layers of rock which make up the ground. Look for places where the ground has been dug up, such as road works, foundations for new buildings, railway cuttings, quarries or river banks, to see for yourself what you have noticed on the map. Go with an adult and be careful. These are dangerous places. Ask a geologist at your local museum about the building materials that are linked to the geology of your area.

**HOW CAN YOU TELL?**
- look at aerial photographs
- study a geology map of your area
- look at a street map of your town

**This aerial photograph of Marlow on the River Thames shows how the flat land beside the river is well-suited to farming.**

## Building materials

Before the railways were built in the middle of the nineteenth century, most people built their houses out of local materials, such as **flint** from the fields, pebbles from the beach, clay for bricks and tiles from local brickfields, stone or slate from local quarries, or thatch from reeds in ponds. This is why buildings were different in different parts of the country. After the railways were built, in the nineteenth century, building materials could be carried great distances, so that slate from Wales was used to mend and build roofs all over the country.

## Town patterns

Look at the pattern of your town's streets on a modern street map. If the streets are narrow and higgledy-piggledy, they may be medieval. If the map is set out in a grid pattern, the streets could be Georgian (1714-1830), or belong to a new town built after the Second World War (1939-45). Modern towns have wide, straight roads so that cars, buses and heavy lorries can pass through easily.

▲ **This old house and bridge in Ambleside, Westmorland, were built from the stone that is found in the area.**

**This modern map of Uckfield shows the pattern of the newer streets.**

# Public buildings

Some towns grew up because there were industries, such as mining, quarrying or brickmaking, which had attracted people to the area. Were there industries like these in your town? You could look for the sites of these industries in the oldest street directory you can find in your library, and plot them on a modern street map of your town. Do the same industries exist today, or are the original buildings now used for something else? Today, even the most recently-built industrial estates are being converted to other uses, for example to offices or superstores.

**These quarrymen from Blaenau Ffestiniog in Wales were photographed in 1900.**

During the Industrial Revolution, in the nineteenth century, many new industries were set up and people moved from the countryside to the towns to work in the factories. The banks and public buildings in your town may have been built around this time. Town halls were built for the new **town councils**. They were somewhere for councillors to meet and discuss how the town should be organized, and for the officials, who carried out their decisions, to work. Try to visit your town hall. It may be richly decorated, reflecting the pride the people felt in their town. Libraries and museums are public buildings too. They were often built by local merchants, to show their wealth.

**WHAT TO LOOK FOR:**
- what were the first industries in your area?
- how old is your town hall?
- when was your local railway station built?

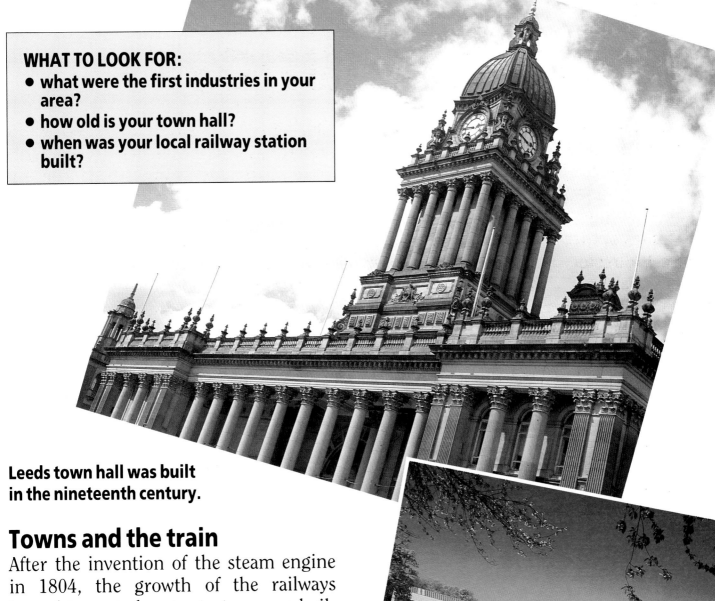

Leeds town hall was built in the nineteenth century.

## Towns and the train

After the invention of the steam engine in 1804, the growth of the railways brought great changes to towns and villages all over Britain. Towns that were on a railway line became very successful and soon nearly every town in the country was linked by train. Many stations were built. Some were huge and decorated whilst others were more cosy.

The invention of the motor car in 1885 made train travel less popular. Cars became cheap enough for many people to own one. Today fewer people choose to travel by train and many railways have had to close. You may be able to find some old stations that are now restaurants, offices or houses.

You can see from this modern museum in Glasgow how different today's building styles are from those in the past.

# Leisure time

Many buildings are places where people meet to eat or drink, to enjoy themselves, or to play or to listen to music.

Over the years, places of entertainment are quite often changed, or even converted to other uses, as popular pastimes change. Large-scale maps, which you can find in your reference library, will show how the local parks were laid out. Make a tracing of the parks marked on the 25 inch-to-the-mile 1893 **Ordnance Survey map**. Then try to draw the layout of the park as it is today over the top. What changes can you see? Perhaps there was a bandstand in 1893, but there may not have been a children's playground or public tennis courts. What does this tell you about changes in the way people spend their leisure time?

**Plot existing hotels, restaurants, cafés, pubs, theatres, concert halls, cinemas, parks and playgrounds on an up-to-date street map, to make your own leisure map. Is there a skating rink, a swimming pool, a sports centre, a dry ski slope, a golf course, a multiplex, a take-away, or a radio or television station in your area? Have you remembered to plot them on your map?**

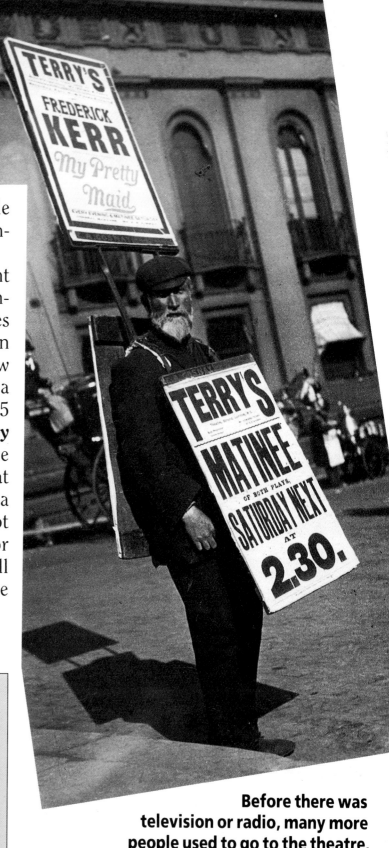

**Before there was television or radio, many more people used to go to the theatre.**

22

Which entertainments, fashionable in the past, are still fashionable today and which have disappeared? Newspapers can tell you what was going on at a particular date. You can compare past editions with a modern paper. Your local library may also have a collection of old theatre posters or postcards. The library, or junk shops, may have old guidebooks which will show you how entertainment and hotels in holiday places have changed. Before the invention of the wireless, the gramophone, cinema and television, there was only live entertainment.

**On another street map, plot the places of entertainment which have disappeared over the years. To find out what these are, look at different street directories about ten years apart in date. Starting from the earliest directory, mark the buildings which first appear in that directory, using different coloured pens for each year. This will show you what kinds of entertainment were fashionable at different dates.**

**These wooden hoops are very simple compared to modern toys, but the girls are still enjoying themselves.**

# Schools

You might want to try to find out what school life was like in the past, and what was different for pupils then. If your school is in a new building, you may want to find out about the building it replaced. Perhaps there are pictures of the old building. The old school may have been pulled down, or it may have been converted to a new use. Even if it is no longer used as a school, it will be worth having a look at the building for clues about the past.

Many schools were built in the second half of the nineteenth century, when laws were passed making education **compulsory** for children. If your school is in an old building, it may date from this time. What material was used to build the school? It may be built of stone if it is in an area where stone was quarried, otherwise it will probably be built of brick. The windows will be high up, to stop pupils being distracted from their lessons by looking at interesting things going on outside.

**Does your school have high windows like this one, or is the building more modern?**

**WHAT ARE THE CLUES?**
- **is the school building old or new?**
- **what is it built of?**
- **is there a coal shed or air raid shelter in the playground?**
- **are the windows high up?**
- **does the school have any old slates or desks?**

▲ These girls are learning how to look after their teeth. How is the classroom different from yours?

Would you guess that this seventeenth-century building was once a school? ▼

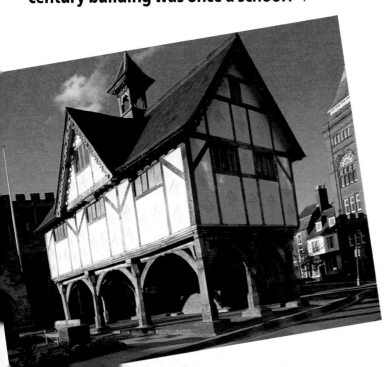

In the past, boys and girls were kept apart at school. Perhaps you can find the words 'Boys' and 'Girls' over separate entrances. There could be separate playgrounds and cloakrooms too. Can you find the old coal shed in the playground, or an air raid shelter from the Second World War? There might be an open air shelter in the playground which would have been used to play in when the weather was bad. Old schools do not usually have playing fields, as sport was not thought to be important until the beginning of this century.

## On the inside

Has your school kept an old desk or slate? Ask your head teacher whether she or he has the old school log book, which is a record of what happened in the school. The old school registers will tell you where pupils moved on to when they left, and what their parents did for a living.

Perhaps you could invite some old pupils or teachers to come and tell you about their time at your school.

25

This picture from around 1480 shows a merchant bargaining with a customer. People still bargain in markets today.

# Shops

Markets and fairs used to be the most important places to buy and sell goods and exchange news. They started many centuries ago and grew as the towns grew. Fairs took place on particular days each year, and markets on a particular day of the week. **Hawkers** would walk about crying their **wares**. Street names, for example Cheapside, give us clues to the places where markets were held.

When was the first shop built in your area, and what did it sell? Check in the early trade directories for shops and markets. The early directories told buyers and sellers where to find each other, so that they could trade their goods. Compare the trades found in one directory in one year with the trades in the directory five or ten years later. This will tell you which trades flourished and which trades

**WHERE TO LOOK:**
- check street names for clues to fairs and markets
- look at early trade directories for changes in trades
- has the fascia board or shop front been changed?
- are there any old signs or adverts outside?
- can you find a mosaic outside?

died out. The names of some trades have changed over the centuries. What did drapers, milliners and haberdashers sell?

## Facelifts

Sometimes you might notice the **fascia** board above a shop being changed. Look to see if the original fascia is visible underneath, and take a photo of it if you can. You can tell what a shop used to sell from different clues. High up on the side of the building you may see a painted wall sign, an advertisement, or a carved symbol, for example a cow if the building was once a dairy. Don't forget to look at the ground for historical evidence too. Sometimes you will see the old name of a shop in a **mosaic** pavement in front of it. Remember shopping streets are busy with people and traffic – be careful.

Changes to shops are taking place all the time. Did you know that, in the last quarter of a century, the population in villages has increased, yet the number of shops has decreased? Many supermarkets are now built on the edges of towns. As so many people now own cars, they can go further away to shop, and buy more food less often. Where do you think most elderly people and families without cars buy their food?

**This is WH Smith & Sons in Finchley, London, in 1895. How is it different from a modern shop?**

# New uses for old buildings

Make a list of the buildings in your high street. Check them in the most recent street and trade directories, probably from the mid-1970s. Has the use of any of the buildings changed? Go back and look at the buildings again to see if you can see any evidence of their previous use. You might see a name etched in the glass of a window, a wide opening leading to a paved yard, or pointed windows in a building which reminds you of a church.

If you walk around a historic town, you will see many buildings whose use has changed over the years. There are shops that have become houses, and houses that have become shops. Old cinemas and theatres are often used as bingo halls. Schools, stations and churches may have been turned into houses or flats. There might be a **warehouse**, factory or shops that are now offices. A **forge** may have become a garage, a manor house might now be a hotel. Nowadays some people

How might you guess
that this Youth Hostel was once a friary?

**Only the notice above the door saying 'Licensed to sell game' tells you that this coffee house was once a butcher's shop.**

live in buildings which were once meant to shelter animals, such as barns and stables.

Look for clues that a building has changed its use. You might see blocked up windows or an archway which look out of place. Keep an eye open for the unexpected and unexplained.

You may discover many clues that you did not notice on your first inspection: a curved wall leading to a yard, scrape marks on the side of a building, a carved symbol just under the roof, or an unexpected name, such as Viaduct Court or Station Cottages where no railway exists. Would that make you curious?

You could carry on looking back through the street and trade directories from every five years, to find other changes of use further back in time.

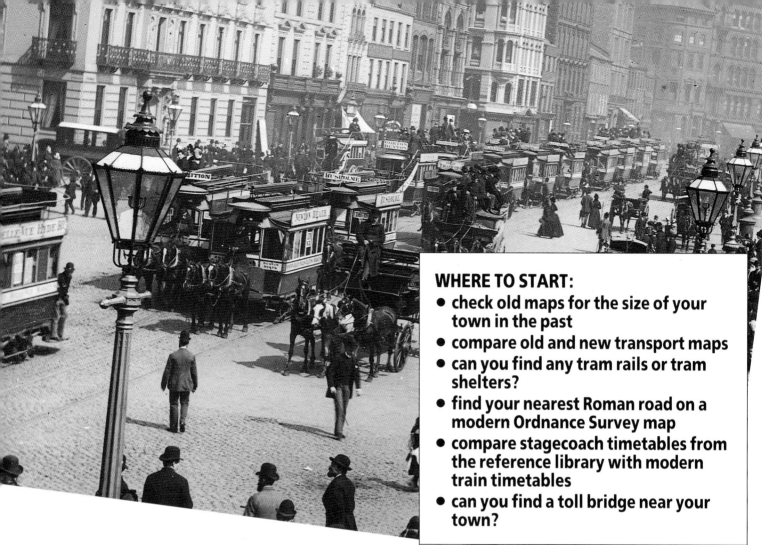

**WHERE TO START:**
- check old maps for the size of your town in the past
- compare old and new transport maps
- can you find any tram rails or tram shelters?
- find your nearest Roman road on a modern Ordnance Survey map
- compare stagecoach timetables from the reference library with modern train timetables
- can you find a toll bridge near your town?

The route of the rails for these horse buses in Manchester is now used by the city centre's new Metro train.

# Travel and transport

The invention of different kinds of transport will have affected the shape and size of the place where you live. In the past, towns and villages were small, as people walked everywhere or used horses. They had to live near the place where they worked.

Horse buses were the first type of public transport in towns, followed by electric trams, trolley buses and motor buses. You might find some old transport maps in the library. These show the routes of roads, canals, railways, trams and buses. Can you find a tram shelter or tram rails in your town?

The invention of trains and cars allowed people to live out in the suburbs, or even the countryside, and **commute** to work. Towns are now linked by fast motorways and railways, so that people can live hundreds of kilometres from where they work.

# Out of town

Have you ever travelled along an ordinary road that went on for many kilometres in a straight line? If you have, the road could well have been following the route of one of the first main roads across England. These were built by the Romans, to move their armies and goods around more easily.

Motorists are sometimes charged a sum of money, or a toll, to use bridges or tunnels. During the eighteenth century, the main **turnpike** roads were looked after by groups of men who charged travellers tolls to use them, in return for keeping the roads in good repair. A spiked bar marked the beginning and end of the stretch of road managed by these **trustees**. Stagecoach companies ran regular services on turnpike roads, changing horses at coaching inns about ten miles (16km) apart. Journeys that would now take you a few hours, in a car, used to take people days to travel.

Before the invention of railways, it was difficult to carry heavy loads overland, especially in winter. Sometimes merchants transported goods by river or sea. In the eighteenth century, canals were built to move goods to and from factories by horse-drawn **barge**. In the nineteenth century, steam trains soon became faster than barges and coaches, and became the most popular way to travel. Today it is possible for business people to fly to a meeting hundreds of kilometres away, then fly home again within a few hours.

Compare maps of your town before and after the railway was built. Has the town changed? Collect modern transport maps from your railway and bus stations. Does each company have its own map? Compare them to old transport maps to see if there are many more routes now.

Before the train was invented, canals were used to transport goods.

# Churches and chapels

Today there are many different religions in Britain, that have come from different parts of the world. **Mosques** and **synagogues** are found in many towns, as well as Sikh, Buddhist and Hindu communities. In the past, however, most people in Britain were Christians. This is why most old churches are Christian churches, even though the people living near them now may not be Christians.

An old church is useful to the local historian, because it holds many clues to the history of the local community. Quite often, the oldest building you can find will be a church. Why is it built where it is? Are there any mysterious lumps and bumps in the ground surrounding it? They may be signs of an earlier church or village.

Any changes to a church can tell you about changes in the town. If a church was enlarged, it probably happened when the town was growing. Sometimes a church has been made smaller, and you can find evidence of **aisles** which are no longer there. Why might the **congregation** have decreased when it did?

**Stained glass windows are made from pieces of coloured glass that are joined together by lead strips to make a picture.**

**NORMAN**
**(c. AD 1200)**
North aisle and chapel added to Saxon building

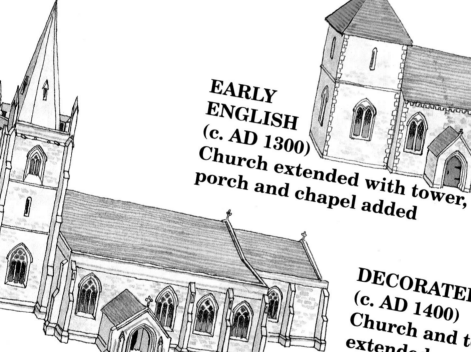

**EARLY ENGLISH**
**(c. AD 1300)**
Church extended with tower, porch and chapel added

**DECORATED**
**(c. AD 1400)**
Church and tower extended, with south aisle added

# A Parish Church

Churches from different times look different, so you can tell roughly how old they are, although some later churches can trick you because they imitate churches of the past. Your clues are the arches, the **mouldings** and the windows. An old church may have arches, mouldings and windows of different styles, but there may be a guide book, which will tell you when each part was built.

# Church styles

Many of the oldest churches in Britain were built by the Saxons (450-1066) or the Normans (1066-1200). Saxon churches were usually wooden, but most that survive are of stone. Both the Saxons and the Normans built church windows and roofs with rounded arches, although some Saxon churches have windows shaped like an upside-down 'V'. The windows were narrow, without glass, and there weren't many of them, so the churches were often dark inside.

**An Early English window (c. 1200–1300)**

**A Norman window (c. 1066–1200)**

Around AD 1200, builders discovered how to build pointed arches, and churches became larger. In the twelfth and thirteenth centuries, pointed arches were used for the stone **vaulting** that replaced wooden roofs, and for the **buttresses** outside churches that strengthened the walls. Windows were often slits, grouped together in twos. This is called the Early English style and lasted for about one hundred years.

**A Decorated window (c. 1300–1400)**

Ask the vicar whether you may take rubbings of the lettering and drawings on the gravestones and memorial brasses. Use soft paper and a soft wax crayon.

Churches in the Decorated style (1300-1400) had tall, wide windows that contained brightly-coloured glass. The stonework was decorated with carvings. Builders then became more skilled and built bigger churches, which looked very upright, or perpendicular, and had large windows. This is called the Perpendicular style (1400-1500).

The windows of this period were tall, with a pointed or flat-pointed arch. The buttresses were often given **pinnacles**, and towers were built on top of the corners, to make the churches seem taller.

**A Perpendicular window
(c. 1400–1500)**

Between the years from 1500 to 1800, some churches were built in the Classical style. Classical churches looked like large rooms with a **gallery** and a large **pulpit**. They imitated the temples of Ancient Greece and Rome. Many Classical churches were built by Sir Christopher Wren to replace churches destroyed in the Fire of London in 1666. They were designed so that the preacher could be heard everywhere in the church.

In the eighteenth century, galleries were added to some churches. Many new churches were built with galleries already in place. In the nineteenth century, when the population of Britain doubled, the Victorians continued to build churches and **chapels**. Most of them imitated older buildings. Churches built in the twentieth century have also imitated the styles of the past. Today many new churches are built to be used as community centres, where people who live in the area can meet.

**The Classical dome of St Paul's Cathedral is one of the most famous landmarks in London.**

**You can see the small buttresses jutting out of the walls of this Sussex church. A larger church would need larger buttresses.**

## Names and numbers

Sometimes it is possible to trace the families that have lived in an area, by looking at the names on memorials inside a church and on gravestones outside. Only wealthy families could afford memorials, so their names are usually inside the church. However, the names of rich and poor families will be recorded on war memorials.

Your local church may no longer be used. Sometimes the congregation has disappeared, because most of the houses in the area are now shops or offices. Today fewer people go to church, so one vicar may look after two or three churches in a joint **parish**. The people in the joint parish worship at a different church every week.

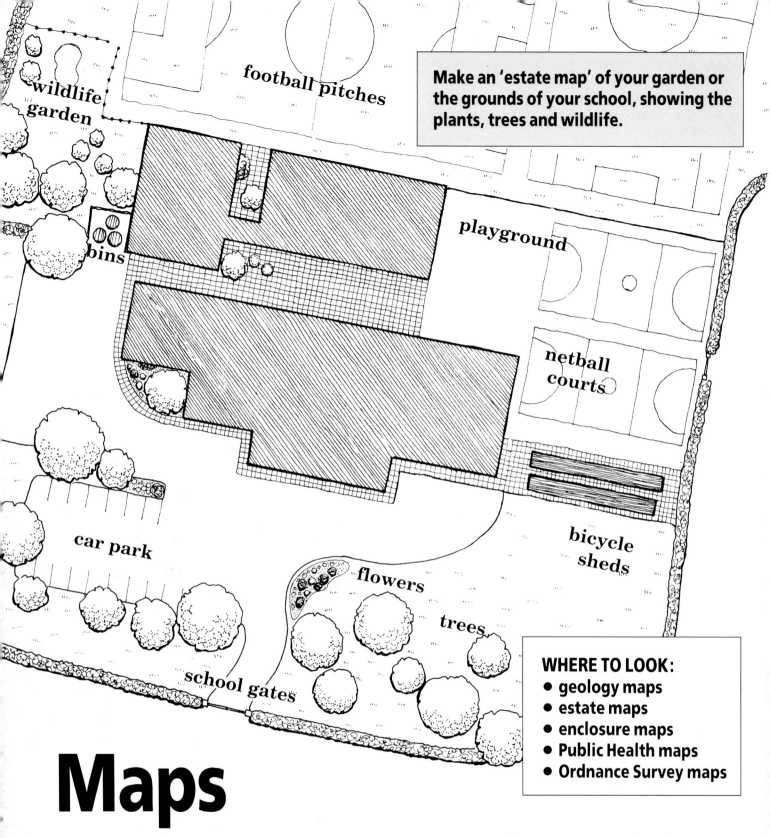

wildlife garden

football pitches

**Make an 'estate map' of your garden or the grounds of your school, showing the plants, trees and wildlife.**

playground

bins

netball courts

car park

bicycle sheds

flowers

trees

school gates

**WHERE TO LOOK:**
- geology maps
- estate maps
- enclosure maps
- Public Health maps
- Ordnance Survey maps

# Maps

Geological maps tell you about the rocks and soil under your feet, but other maps tell different tales. A collection of maps of one place, made at different dates, will show how that place has grown.

**Estate** maps recorded a landowner's estate. They often showed tiny details, such as gardens with shrubs, ponds and vegetables. Some even showed rabbits eating lettuces in the kitchen garden.

Enclosure maps show the changes in farming when open land was enclosed with hawthorn hedges and ditches, to make fields. An Award was drawn up with each map. This was a list of field names with their sizes. It also listed the name of the owner of the land before the changes, and who the new owner was. The fields were often named after their new owner, or something special in the landscape.

Ordnance Survey maps date from the early nineteenth century and show field boundaries, houses and roads. Different maps are drawn to different scales.

After the **Public Health Act** of 1848, some Public Health maps showed wells, wash houses, **sewer grates, privies, dung pits** and **piggeries**, as well as summer houses and garden paths. You can see who had to share a well or privy.

**This map of Brighton marks the town's public buildings and gardens, and the direction of the winds that are common there.**

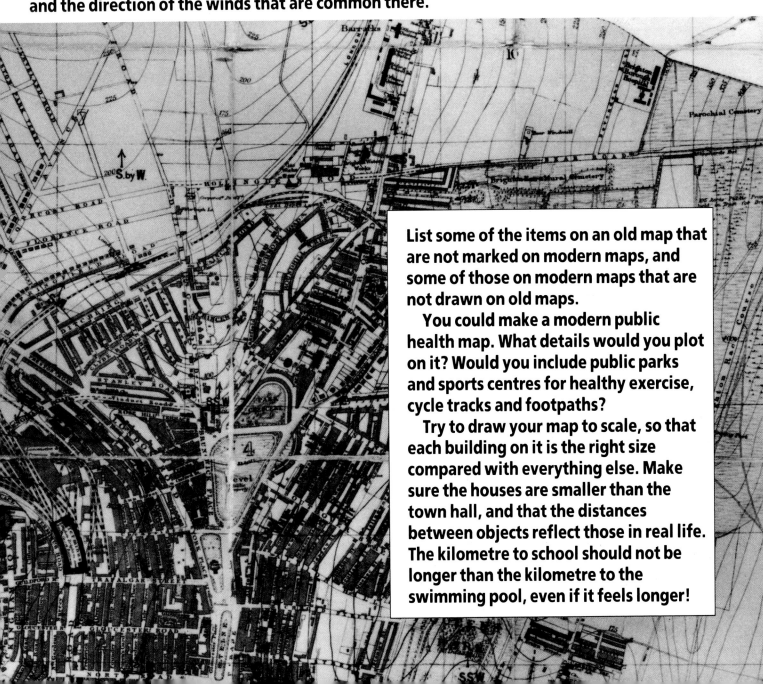

List some of the items on an old map that are not marked on modern maps, and some of those on modern maps that are not drawn on old maps.

You could make a modern public health map. What details would you plot on it? Would you include public parks and sports centres for healthy exercise, cycle tracks and footpaths?

Try to draw your map to scale, so that each building on it is the right size compared with everything else. Make sure the houses are smaller than the town hall, and that the distances between objects reflect those in real life. The kilometre to school should not be longer than the kilometre to the swimming pool, even if it feels longer!

These people will never forget the day when a bomb exploded outside their air raid shelter during the Second World War.

# Oral history

You can also find out about history from people's memories. Your parents and grandparents will remember events that happened before you were born.

You could ask people to tell you about their childhood. What are the most important differences between their childhood and yours? You could also ask old people for the stories their parents and grandparents told them when they were young. By using these 'secondary memories' you could cover over a century. This is called 'oral history' because it comes from the spoken word.

Oral history shows ordinary people that they are part of history. The art of oral history is to draw out memories from the person you are interviewing.

## Down memory lane

Most elderly people can tell interesting stories about the past. Ask them to tell you about their ancestors. You will probably get different stories from different members of the same family. Ask them to tell you about the great events in their lives. Do they remember the Second World War or the first landing on the moon? They will probably have had different experiences in different places, and this will affect their feelings about what happened.

You may find it easier to get people to talk if you play them an old song, or interview two old people together. You could also show them a photograph or something they used when they were young.

**Old photographs show how clothes have changed.**

Not all oral evidence is accurate. You may not understand something, and people sometimes idealize their life in the past. Try to find a way to check the information you have collected in an interview. Maybe check street names in a street directory, or people's names by asking another member of your family.

The best way to record oral history is with a tape recorder. You could practise interviewing a friend first. Write down some questions you want to ask in a notebook before you go, but be prepared to think up new questions while you are listening to the replies. Write up the interview from the tape afterwards.

**Perhaps you know someone who can remember the day when King George V was crowned in 1911?**

# Getting everything together

By now, you will probably know what area you want to study, but try to pick a subject for which the evidence is not too hard to find.

When you have chosen your subject, you could try to find a book about it in the public library. Read the book and follow any notes at the bottom of the pages like a detective. Use the bibliography, or list of books to read on the same subject at the end, to find further trails.

The library may have a local history card index, computer database or microfiche catalogue (small sheets of film that list books and newspapers) that will help you. If you do not know how to use these catalogues, or where to go next for information, ask the librarian for help.

You will also find guides, directories, cuttings collections, maps, photographs, postcards, documents and people's scrapbooks in the library. You may find old tickets, and theatre or football programmes at jumble sales or in junk shops. You might collect modern ones to compare with these. They will be interesting in a few years' time.

Directories include descriptions of your town. If you live in a tourist town, compare what the directories and tourist guides say – they might be quite different. Directories also list local newspapers, timetables, and churches. They tell you about workshops and factories, and will help you trace the growth of your town.

Newspapers and magazines can be very useful. Sometimes there are advertisements with amusing pictures which you could photocopy and keep. Old school magazines can give you evidence about your school.

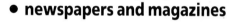

**HELPLINE**
- books from the public library
- bibliographies and footnotes
- a local history card index, computer database or microfiche catalogue
- guides, directories, cuttings, maps, photographs, postcards, entertainment programmes
- newspapers and magazines

When you are taking notes in the library, always write down the name and page number of the book, directory or magazine in which you have found your evidence. Otherwise you can waste a lot of time looking for it again if you want to check it. A good historian will always write down where any information comes from, so that no-one will think it is a story he or she has made up. The evidence you find will provide you with many interesting stories.

# Timeline

| | |
|---|---|
| 1086 | **Domesday Book**, a register of the land of England, was made. |
| 1348 | An illness called bubonic plague, known as the Black Death, arrived in England and killed about a quarter of the population. |
| 1600 | Population of Britain just over 4 million. |
| 1665 | The Great Plague. |
| 1666 | The Fire of London. |
| 1700 | Population of Britain 5 million. |
| 1759 | Josiah Wedgwood opened his first pottery at Burslem. |
| 1796 | Edward Jenner invented a vaccination against smallpox. |
| 1801 | The first census. Population of Britain 8 million. |
| 1804 | Richard Trevithick built the first steam locomotive. |
| 1829 | Robert Peel set up the Metropolitan Police force. |
| 1834 | The Poor Law set up workhouses, where people without homes or jobs could live in return for doing unpaid work. |
| 1837 | Queen Victoria came to the throne. |
| 1840 | The first postage stamps came into use. |
| 1850s | The first post boxes were built. |
| 1851 | Census showed just over half Britain's population (of 20 million) lived in towns. |
| 1854 | A cholera epidemic led to demands for a clean water supply and proper sewage systems in the big cities. |
| 1863 | The opening of the first London Underground Railway. The foundation of the Football Association. |
| 1868 | The last public hanging. |
| 1869 | The first Sainsbury's shop opened in Drury Lane, London. |
| 1876 | Alexander Graham Bell invented the telephone. Primary education was made compulsory. |
| 1877 | The first public electric lighting in London. |
| 1887 | The invention of the gramophone. |
| 1895 | Guglielmo Marconi invented wireless telegraphy. |

| 1901 | Population of Britain 40 million. |
| 1908 | The first old age pension. |
| 1909 | Blériot became the first person to fly across the English Channel. |
| 1914–18 | The First World War. Compulsory military service and food rationing were brought in. |
| 1920 | The first public radio broadcast in Pittsburgh, USA. |
| 1929 | The first BBC television programme. |
| 1939–45 | The Second World War. Bombing of British cities, compulsory military service, evacuation and rationing began. |
| 1940 | The drug Penicillin was first used. |
| 1945 | The creation of the Welfare State introduced social security payments for the unemployed. |
| 1946 | The New Towns Act led to the creation of the first new towns. |
| 1947 | The Town and Country Planning Act made it illegal for people to change buildings or land without permission. |
| 1948 | The National Health Service was set up. |
| 1950 | Sainsbury's opened their first supermarket. |
| 1951 | Population of Britain 50 million. |
| 1952 | Queen Elizabeth II came to the throne. |
| 1952–59 | The first high-rise blocks of flats were built at Roehampton, London. |
| 1955 | Commercial television began. |
| 1960 | The first motorway, the M1, was opened. |
| 1967 | Colour television first appeared. |
| 1972 | Satellite television was used for the first time. |
| 1973 | Capital Radio and other local radio stations were set up. |
| 1974 | The Health and Safety at Work Act improved conditions at work. |
| 1978 | The Sony Walkman Personal Stereo appeared. Louise Brown, the first test-tube baby, was born. |
| 1982 | The Falklands War. The first CD players were introduced by Sony. |
| 1985 | A survey showed that around half the homes in Britain had a video recorder, a higher number than in the USA. |
| 1991 | The Gulf War. |

# Glossary

**Aerial photographs** photographs of a place taken from an aircraft above it.

**Aisles** walkways between the seats inside churches.

**Asphalt** a mixture of bitumen, pitch, sand and gravel, used for road surfaces.

**Barge** a flat-bottomed canal boat used for carrying goods.

**Bollards** short posts.

**Boundary stones** stones used to mark the limit of a town or village.

**Buttresses** stone supports outside a building, built to prop up the wall.

**Casement windows** windows that open, like a door.

**Centuries** periods of one hundred years.

**Chapels** small churches that do not have a parish.

**Coaching inn** an inn where stagecoaches could have fresh horses harnessed to them.

**Commute** to travel a distance to and from work.

**Compulsory** something that has to be done, by law.

**Congregation** the people who come together to worship in a church.

**Decades** periods of ten years.

**Detached** standing on its own.

**Domesday Book** a record of the lands of England made for King William I in 1085.

**Dung pits** pits used for storing manure.

**Estate** a large area of land belonging to one family.

**Etched** scratched into something.

**Fascia** the name-board on a shop front.

**Flint** a type of stone found in chalk.

**Forge** a blacksmith's workshop where horses have horseshoes fitted to their hooves.

**Foundry** a workshop for making metal objects.

**Gallery** a balcony running around the inside of a building.

**Geology** the study of the rocks under the ground.

**Georgian** dating from the reign of Kings George I-IV (1714-1830).

**Hawkers** pedlars, or people who travelled about selling goods.

**Lintels** beams of wood across the tops of windows and doors.

**Market garden** an area of land used for growing vegetables and fruit which are to be sold.

**Mews** a yard or street of houses which were once stables.

**Middle Ages** the name given to the period of British history between the years AD 1000-1500.

**Mosaic** a pattern made from small pieces of coloured stone or glass.

**Mosques** places where Muslims come together to worship.

**Mouldings** shapes used to decorate the stonework of buildings.

**Multiplex** a building with several cinema screens, all showing different films.

**Neighbourhood** the area of a town which the people who live there think of as a community.

**Ordnance Survey map** an official, detailed map.

**Parish** a community which has its own church.

**Piggeries** places used for keeping pigs.

**Pinnacles** points, or spires, built on top of walls or towers.

**Privies** lavatories.

**Public Health Act** one of a number of acts passed in the nineteenth century in order to make places more healthy.

**Pulpit** a raised platform used by a preacher in a church.

**Regency** dating from the years 1811-20 when George III was ill and his son ruled as Prince Regent.

**Sash windows** windows that open by sliding up and down.

**Scale** the relationship between the size of something in real life and a model or map of it.

**Semi-detached** a house that is joined to another house on one side.

**Setts** blocks put in the road to stop horses slipping.

**Sewer grates** bars across a drain.

**Slate** a grey rock used to make roofs.

**Stuart** dating from when the Stuart family ruled England (1603-1714)

**Suburb** houses on the edge of a town.

**Symmetrical** the same on both sides.

**Synagogues** places where Jews come together to worship.

**Tarmac** small stones, bound with tar, used for road surfaces.

**Tethering posts** posts to which animals were tied.

**Town councils** groups of people who are chosen to run towns.

**Tram** an electric bus that runs on rails.

**Trustees** the people who are trusted to run something, for example a business, for other people.

**Tudor** dating from when the Tudor family ruled England (1485-1603).

**Turnpike** a road on which a toll was collected.

**Vaulting** arches that fit together to make a roof.

**Viaduct** a bridge carrying a road or railway line across a valley.

**Wares** goods for sale.

**Warehouse** a building for storing goods.

**War Memorials** objects made in memory of an event or a person.

# BOOKS TO READ

**For younger readers:**

*Master Maps with Ordnance Survey*, Patricia & Steve Harrison (OS & Holmes McDougall, 1988)

*Evidence Through Maps*, Bill Boyle (Collins Educational, 1988)

*Local Directories*, Bill Boyle (Collins Educational, 1987)

*In My Time*, John Cockcroft (Collins Educational, 1986)

*Thanks for the Memory*, Sallie Purkiss (Collins Educational, 1987)

*History Around You* books 0-4, L.E. Snellgrove (Oliver & Boyd, 1983)

*Buildings*, David Woodlander (Collins Educational, 1988)

*How Towns Grow and Change*, Laurie Bolwell & Cliff Lines (Wayland, 1985)

Try to watch the Domesday interactive video disc, by the BBC about the Domesday Book. Your school or County Records Office may have a copy.

**For older readers:**

*History on Your Doorstep*, J.R. Ravensdale (BBC, 1982)

*House and Home*, Anthony Quiney (BBC, 1986)

# Index

Pages marked in **bold** include illustrations.